I0755951

FINISHING LINE PRESS
www.finishinglinepress.com

Goodbye Eurydice

poems by

Wisteria Deng

Finishing Line Press
Georgetown, Kentucky

Goodbye Eurydice

ISBN 979-8-89990-461-5 First Edition

ACKNOWLEDGMENTS

Eskimo Birds was first published in *Voice and Verse Poetry Magazine.*

Past versions of these poems were first featured in an exhibition at Accent Sisters.

Poems in this book were written over the past decade. It documents my migration across continents and carries many lives that are not mine alone.

Publisher: Leah Huete de Maines
Editor: Christen Kincaid
Cover Art: Maverick Ran
Author Photo: Jinfeng
Cover Design: Elizabeth Maines McCleavy

Order online: www.finishinglinepress.com
also available on amazon.com

Author inquiries and mail orders:
Finishing Line Press
PO Box 1626
Georgetown, Kentucky 40324
USA

Contents

Eskimo Birds

When they were still husband and wife,
they travelled south
to the sea
to see
migrating birds that travelled halfway
across the earth.
Their wings a thin coat
of the northern light.
He imagined those birds drifting
from small arctic villages where
people make love on soaked fur,
to red regimes of the north where
            a girl with lotus tattoo on her waist
touched herself in front of a mirror
before disappeared.

The same birds landed here—
his tropical island
his green disease.

He kissed his wife with eyes closed. In the dark
her body started to decay. From the ashes she
gave birth to a thousand feathers,
in them hides a bird hard as the glacial ice.

Most migrating birds lose their way home.

He saw her stripping naked in a mirror,
her choking herself with red cloth over mouth,
someone choking her with red cloth over mouth,
over the phantom eye and dripping hair. Red the color
of love of path of home. Red the color
of danger in the jungle of wrong way of a rigged game
of stop
of turn back
of no way back.

Most migrating birds lost their way home.

He opened his eyes.
The wife handed him a peach.
It was the sweetest peach of the summer.
Its fuzz pricked his lips. Lips still wet
from kissing.
It was the sweetest peach he had ever had.
In a few days he would die
from a dirty bomb which saved him from
the nuclear one not long afterwards.
In a few days birds and other animals
would be killed and the next parasite on earth
would not be able to tell which is which from
the mix-and-match flesh.

But he had had the sweetest peach.

Its juice dripped and stained his red shirt.
A little yellow star floated in the wild sea
lost his way home.

Goodbye Eurydice

You told me to let go.
This poem looks a lot different back then.
I am writing and
rewriting us again.
Still trying to figure out
if you will be right.

Another Rock

After Franz Wright

Hours of train, take me
through a hesitant spring. Its skin
pale. Snow lingers on
like a disease refused to peel.

Riding on the back of Sisyphus,
I brush against a blank canvas. My body
smashes colors into the void
of black hills, of leftover rain
on the sidewalk of a foreign city,
reciting future in past tense.

I feed on lost lives.
Suck the livings out from each village I pass.
Fill me up
with their past life, molded mistakes,
boats covered in plastic along the grey shore,
a lady in white fur kicking over empty beer cans
—two can make a crisp sound.
Someone from afar gets up for a toast.

Sisyphus whispered to me that I will shred
another skin.
One night I looked into the mirror
and saw parts of me fade like receding waves.
I peel the dead off but they linger
on. My shadow grows bigger by the day,
preparing to take my throne.

I wanted to ask him how it feels
to relive the same mistake over
and again, and continue to
roll the damn rock up the hill.
He said he did not know.
He forgot every time.

Who is there to teach me about escape
Memory is a lost game.

Who is there to teach me about dying
The world is filled with people
who have never died.

Three Times Summer Drips onto Me

I. Submerge

A girl in bright red kimono reads in a secondhand bookstore. Her long fingers snatch the espresso mug. Sip, swallow, an ocean swirls low.

Pages get flipped over. Words lifted, leaping onto each other, thrashing their way across the sea. Each time her forearm brushing against the mahogany table goes a wave carrying bits of the night to the shore. Tassels dangle from her ears, translucent wings whispering wishes back into her.

She murmurs something off the book as if to say wash –

Wash over me.

II. Cemetery

Last night the moon caught fire.

Underneath the sober blaze I buried my lips in your hair.

Trembling – us frozen in the flame. I imagined you to be what chilled lava tastes like.

Underneath the sober blaze I lifted my skin to show you
fresh scars, thick flesh, faded shades.

All the while the desert plotted against us. Earth shifted in shape.

In the morning we find a gerbil drowning in the toilet bowl.

Murderous moon. You say,
a bad omen.

III. Ruin

Time is a clown juggling clocks.

When a mistake is made, my fingers slide out of your palm. My rose

disintegrates

into a poem.

Last Peach of the Summer

I leave my body at dawn, after the last peach of a summer and watch
the city sways in the morning wind, a tilted Jenga tower.
At the bus stop a man sits crying I love you into his phone.
On a rooftop, two girls still asleep—their limbs lay over one another,
their hair intertwined. Fire of the winter.
I am an oil-stained feather, a bubble chased by kids barefooted,
an accident—that one flake of glass shot into the air when two trains
crash into each other.

The soft flesh of the last peach, ready to rot.
Exit stage left, a body takes a bow.

Somewhere in the city a new day seeps through the crack.
Somewhere, a trembling hand snatches away another piece of wood,
from the bottom of a wobbling tower.

Summer, Encore

And then you hug me. A summer ends.

Night was a thin cloth dissolving away
Between two lips, time
unfurls like a somber hope.
Beneath your body a torched tundra.
There—
rays of tomorrow leap off the cliff.
Splitting ends of my hair nibble the dawning dew
off our skin.

What cannot hold us—
Dying light of August. Floating dust.
Torn envelopes drenched in the thorny rain.
What cannot hold us breaks
into metallic flakes on my fingernails,
a wedding ring from a vending machine.
What cannot hold us makes
a summer that ends where it begins,
a hug that swallows two bodies
and snarls and hurls and throws up
skins that twist and turn and echo
echo, echo all over
again.

The Two Times I loved you the most in a car

After Dorothea Grossman

Once we stopped on the highway to watch
stars wreaking havoc over us. City lights a quiet riot,
a surrender to fictional freedom.
You whispered don't go home tonight.
Words took roots on my cheek the way spring dampens a feather.

Another time you wrapped your body over mine
outside a roller-skate rink where your son learns his steps
by taking bad falls. I watched him going too fast, failing to
turn every time, instead ramming his body hard into the railing.
All the while heat coming off your neck soaked through my hair.
I rubbed my head against a faded scar on your collarbone
the way an animal marks her scent.

One day I said out of the blue that we have spent most waking time
    together
in the crawl space of a car.
What I didn't say was the times I love you the most when you fix
your eyes on the night roads, a negotiation between two kinds
of darkness. What I didn't say
was the times I pretend to slip into a slumber, knowing you could
have driven me off a cliff.
What I didn't say was after that day outside the rink, an image stuck
    to me
when we fuck—going too fast, missing steps, ramming bodies into
    the railing,
not knowing how to make a turn.

Yellow Light

Decades gash through us.
Through the hole it blew open,
my body sinks inward
—where a ring-shaped rust lies, now
a damp dark tunnel.
In it hides summer mist, drenched whispers
giving way to a goodnight kiss,
a thousand farewells. Thousands
little fires toying my hair.

A thousand farewells. Each a well-crafted
lie. The true goodbye has taken place
way back:
Under the streetlamp your lips
landed on mine, a fleeting, frightened butterfly.
The same yellow light now tears
through the curtain by my deathbed.
A scarf to ward off the years,
now a tight noose around my neck.
We emerged from an ocean where your skin
grazed against mine, our hair
seaweeds, commanding waves to soar,
parting the sky.
The same water now lures us back with its decadent
darkness, cold scents from those crushed pine needles, corpse
of a spring we never had.

Decades hung between us.
At the end of the tunnel flickered yellow light—
A mirage of home, promises of earth made
on the dissolving land.
Was the light coming out of your kitchen?
You holding a slice of grapefruit up to your grandson,
humming a nursery rhyme.
Or was it a warning sign?
In that intersection where I could have taken a right
and found my way back.

The Way Stars Die

All stars die. Ours
explodes above Brooklyn, where young nights
lay open a snare.
Times collapse. The past stumbles down
a flight of stairs.
At once I am a baby wrapped in shroud,
a bride lost all her hair.
My lover pleasures me into the wintry night,
through the same tunnel a foreign hand
drags the stillbirth out between my thighs.

Words expired. I trap sour dreams on paper.
Bringing reverie to life is about control
I want to lose control.

Before Sunrise

"To say goodbye is to die a little."
—Raymond Chandler

An old man with the body of a furless bear
swings your luggage onto the conveyor belt.
His stomach moans as the weighing scale shoots up
a number too high.

Inside hides two towns along the east coast,
six hours of drive with blanched almonds in a
plastic bag shut tight, three separations—
us,   us,   us.
Us dozing off in a Starbucks waiting for your Red Eye—
Two stranded, waiting for ships to sail in the air.
Us leaving an ancient ruin behind—I loosened my grip:
fly blind. Us
collecting airports around the globe, from a tropical dot
soaked in rainy day satay and over-grilled regrets, to
a winter too warm, a hypnotic drive before sunrise.

Your overweight luggage is stuck between
a furless bear and betrayal, between
one rolling wave and the
next. I give the suitcase a final nudge, a push
tipping the boat away
into the sea.
In my hand remains the touch of its rough
edges, the touch
of your half-shaven face
like wet ropes etching into my skin.

Before the sunrise we
part, so I could melt into the night,
swallow the body you left behind.
Before the sunrise a city
gives itself over, gives birth,
gives birth to itself over again.

Before the sunrise I die
a little, just
a little, a little death just
for you.

The Weight of a Whale

You used to keep a whale under the bed,
feeding him half-licked lollipops, rainy day regrets and letters
no longer matter.

In the mornings you woke to the sound of him chewing
on fresh nightmares, his teeth woven wires.

He watched you make love to a pale seaside girl who smelled like
    ginger,
how your finger runs through her like threads in an overtime story,
how she melts just little between you and the next terror.

Before each day he grew into himself, his eyes empty rings
of spring fire, his body shrinking inwards until
it meets the dense callous on a rippling heart.
A song collapsed. He was ready.

One night you carried him on your back and ran
to a lake of drunken moonlight where he takes
flight. On his curves stars skid through and plummet
into the dark water. He swims
to somewhere you cannot see.

You will never fall asleep again
Etched onto your skin
that putrid smell of a dead whale.

White Reunion

Decades hung between us.
Open gash on this night, torn membrane of a dying insect.

Drenched letters. Return to sender.
An island stranded, yearning for shore.

I wrote to you in death, in the smothering smell
of the last lilies. In a burning house. In the age of war.
In a slow slaughter, the crippling camp inside my head, I
wrote to you.
With all my fingers retching tears, eyes slit open lost
years. With half a heart and over pulled skin, through
the wide wounds for a mouth I wrote
I wrote to you.

Decades gash through us.
Instead we talk about those white lilies you brought.
How it trembles in the humming sound of an IV drip.
How it lures in the flies.
How they die on its wide petals, broken wings quivering in the night
as if there left one last flight.

Past Lives

In a wild July we biked along the ocean
Before winds could take shape we watched
flights taking off.
Giant metal bellies brushing
against the water.
For a second I wondered if the bird would sink.

Tell me summer love
—Do you think of our past lives as sinking birds?
Each gives birth to a star as they plummet into earth.
Or are they salt crystals crushed in the retreating waves?

One wave carries away our first house, where letters still
arrive years after our flight: envelopes reigning our names
drenched in the evening rain.
Another compiles our defeat, stories stuck in corners
we will never reach. Coins between couch seats,
coxcomb bulbs caught behind the counter,
take-out chopsticks choked down the drain.

The day we parted ways I cracked a tooth that had been aching
for past a decade. Low buzz of pain like a twilight lullaby,
like the mesmerizing spin of a ceiling fan, humming her way
through every stilt house in this tropical island.

The day we parted ways I cracked a tooth that had been mine
until no longer. Lying flat at the dentist's, I tasted metal sinking
down my throat. A quiet prey, I
allowed long tools to pry me
open. Water rinsed through numbed flesh that
no longer felt like mine.
All I could hear was the sound of waves retreating
inside me. Each splash a past live sinking
beyond my reach.
Each splash a death of us.

Requiem

Remember when we fell asleep together how our hair tangled up
like dying roots like twisted fingers like tongues of a snake
soaking in the blue moonlight.
Outside the city was at war.
Oil burning on water. Men tugging their leather
sheath across the street
leaving a bloody track.

I woke up to the sound of teens lighting up firecrackers
outside the shelter—a thousand whim-wrapped terrors
taking flight.

Maybe that was the moment

or perhaps days later when you danced in red velvet
skin caught fire
I realized I will die
many deaths before mine.

One death riding your bike rubbing my cheekbone
against your oversized shirt bathed in second-hand smoke.
Another when you poured ginger tea into the next
morning, letting out a quiet moan the way leaves tremble
underneath a spring.
And many more hiding in your porcelain eyes

so when the war catches on
I can tell you I know
how this one is gonna end.
We have been through this together
over and again
before it's time.

Rjukan

Couched deep in the valley and submerged in darkness most of the year, its people put up giant mirrors to reflect a tiny slice of the sun onto the town square—an apparition as true as the celestial body of life. This is how I think of you sometimes, and my childhood house you once covered in wisteria vines, since torn down in a hurricane. When we talk, your face from oceans away glistens on my palms and I hear the faintest cry from your neighbor's cat. With sore arms I hold up giant mirrors, pleading to the gods—May I borrow a square of light even in the darkest times of the year.

With Thanks

My deepest gratitude goes to those who have taught me the impossible lesson of letting go—through writing (Leslie Stainton, Cody Walker, Erin Woodford, Joan Kwon Glass, Sam Cha) and through clinical psychology (Mary O'Brien, Christy Olezeski, Dwain Fehon). To my chosen family—Allen, Katherine, Kaye, Aaron, Annie, Melvin and SJ—you are the tethering force that keeps me on this earth.

I give my last note to my parents, even though they will never get to read this. Mom, my life is deeply enriched through you. Thank you for teaching me to care for others and to love myself. Thank you for being my best friend and my closest ally. Thank you for being my rock. Dad, I don't think I have ever written anything without your phantom hidden somewhere on the page. This is one of the many times I will say goodbye to you. I will keep saying it until the day we meet again. I love you.

To the many Eurydice in my life: I will always turn around to look you in the eyes, before losing you over and again. This book is for you, and for others who have also turned to look back, who choose not to let go.

Wisteria Deng is a writer, theater maker, and clinical psychologist in training. *Goodbye Eurydice* is her debut chapbook, shaped by migration, grief, remembrance and return. She is the founding artistic director of Vermilion Theater, an AAPI women-led nonprofit creating multilingual performance and community healing spaces.

www.ingramcontent.com/pod-product-compliance
Lightning Source LLC
LaVergne TN
LVHW090543110826
845146LV00003B/1241

9798899904615